THIS CANDLEWICK BOOK BELONGS TO:

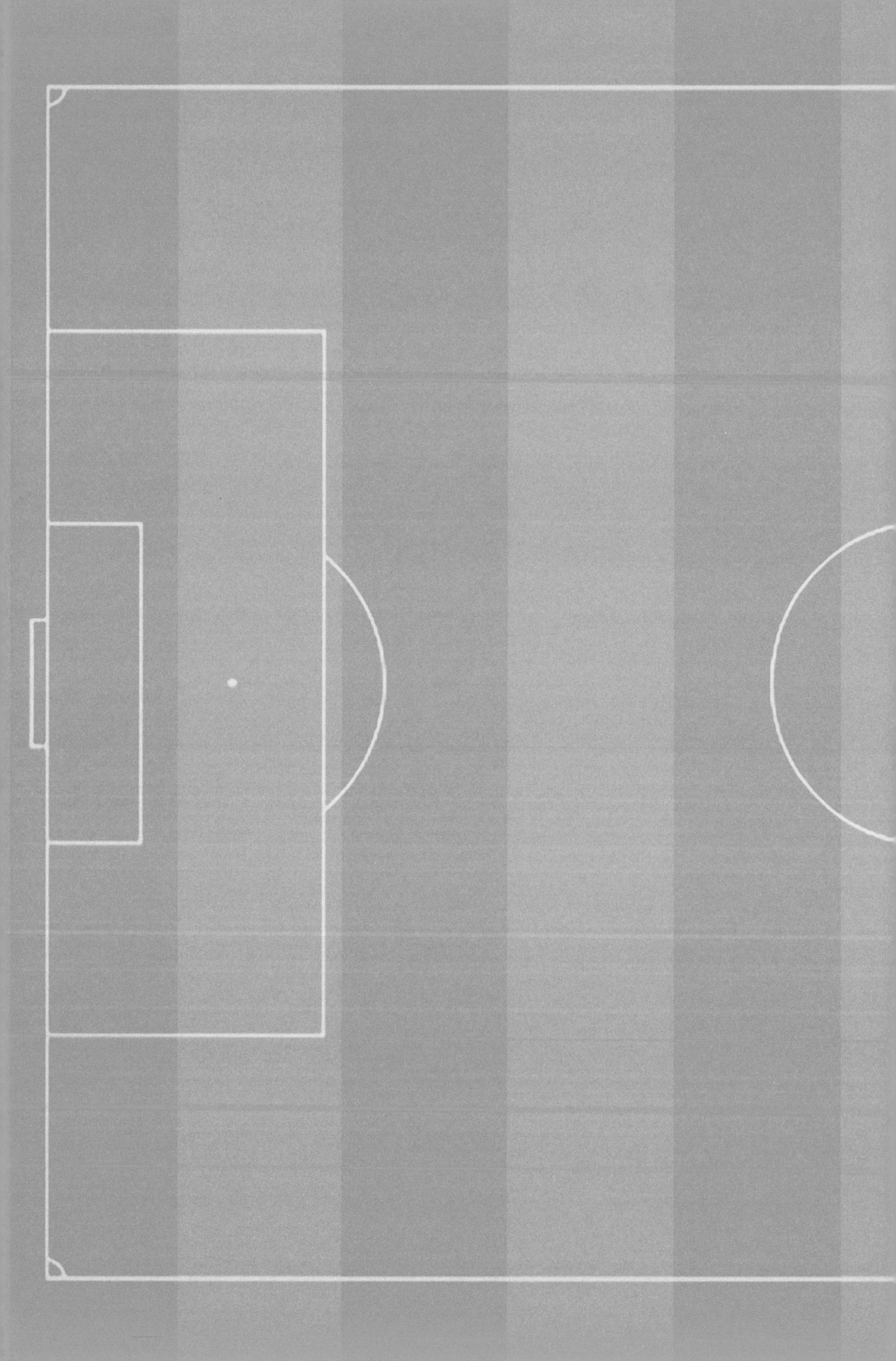

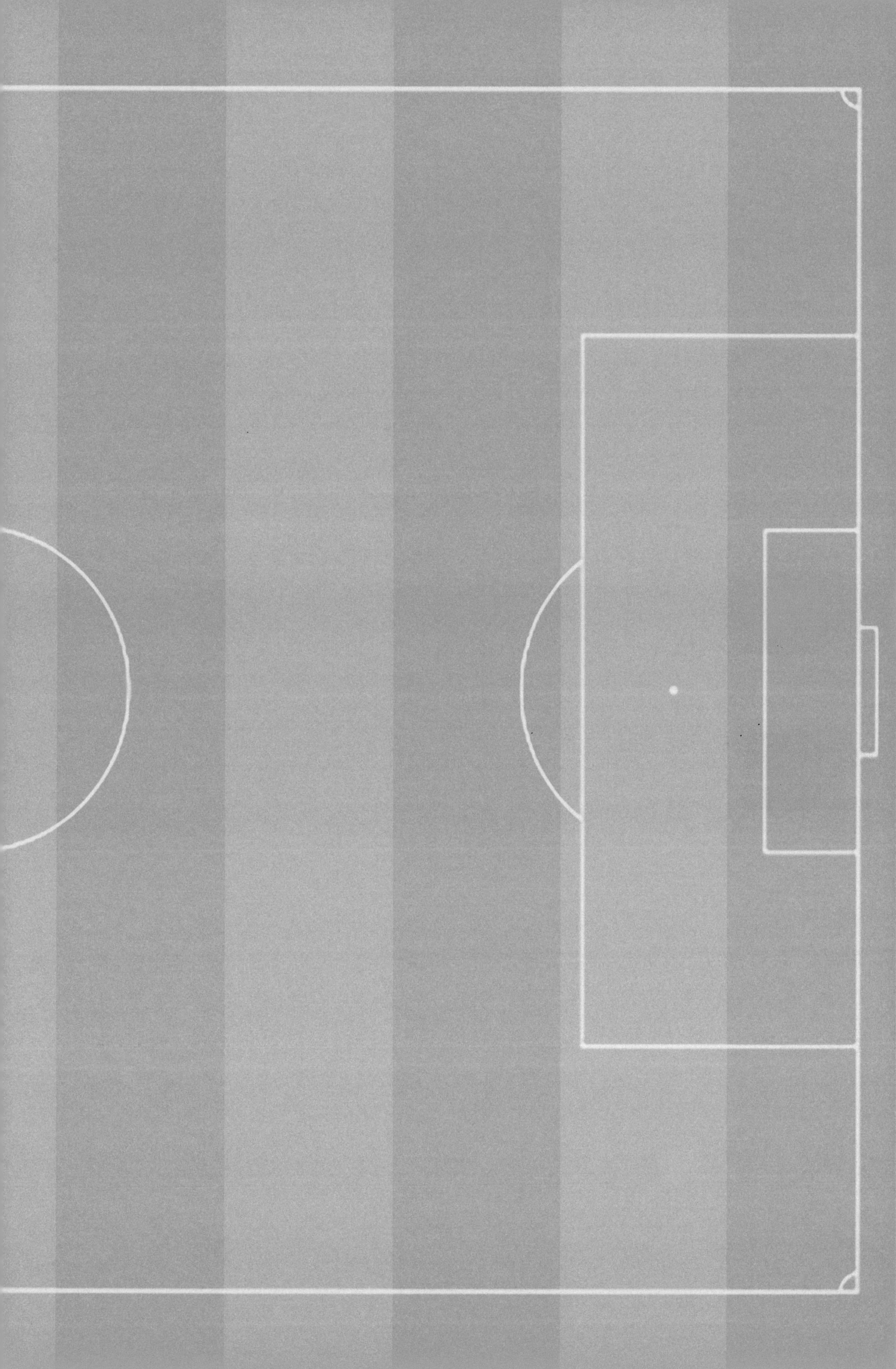

LD

CCER

S

Charles R. Smith Jr.

Candlewick Press

CONTENTS

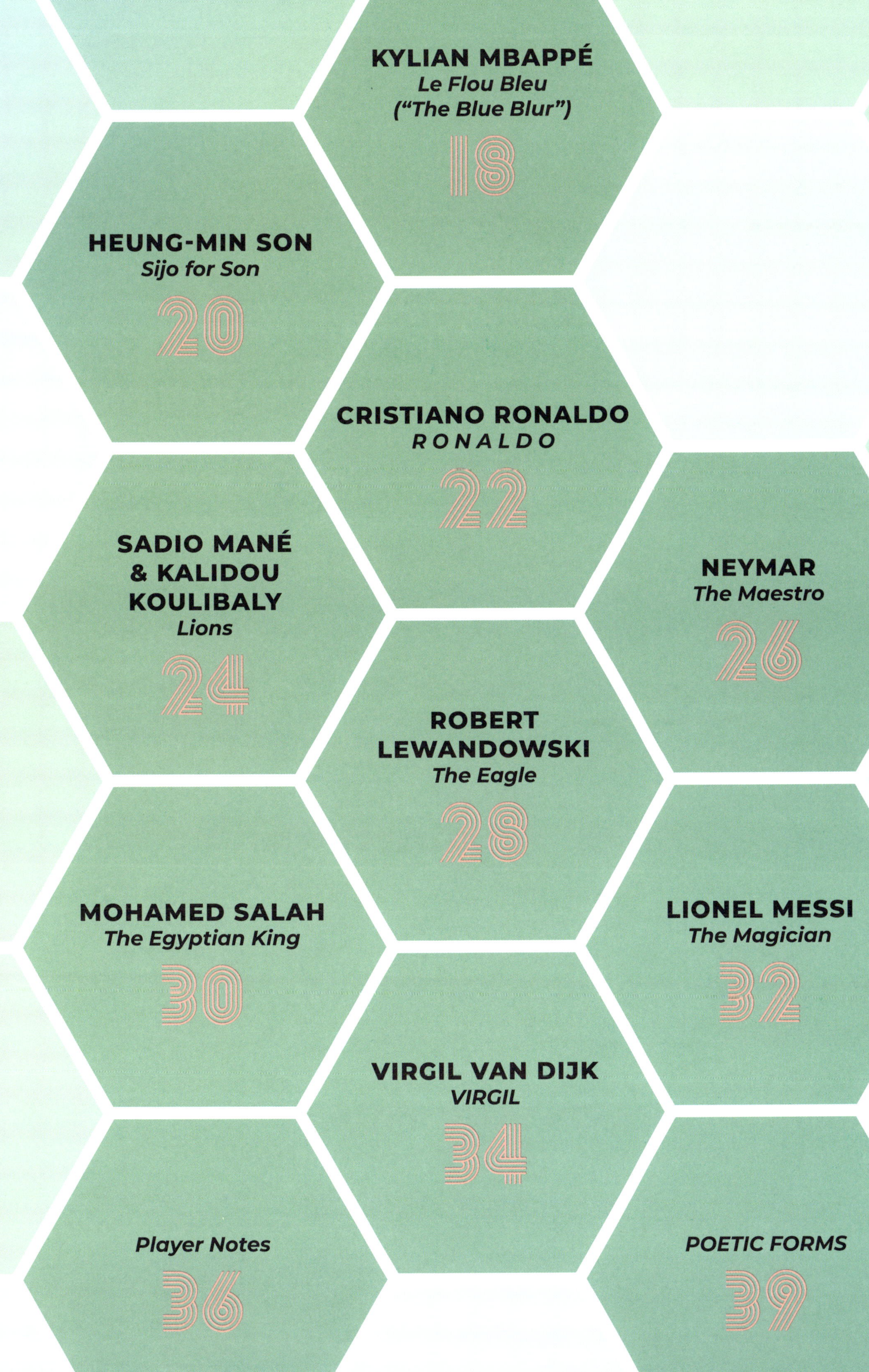

ROAD RUNNER

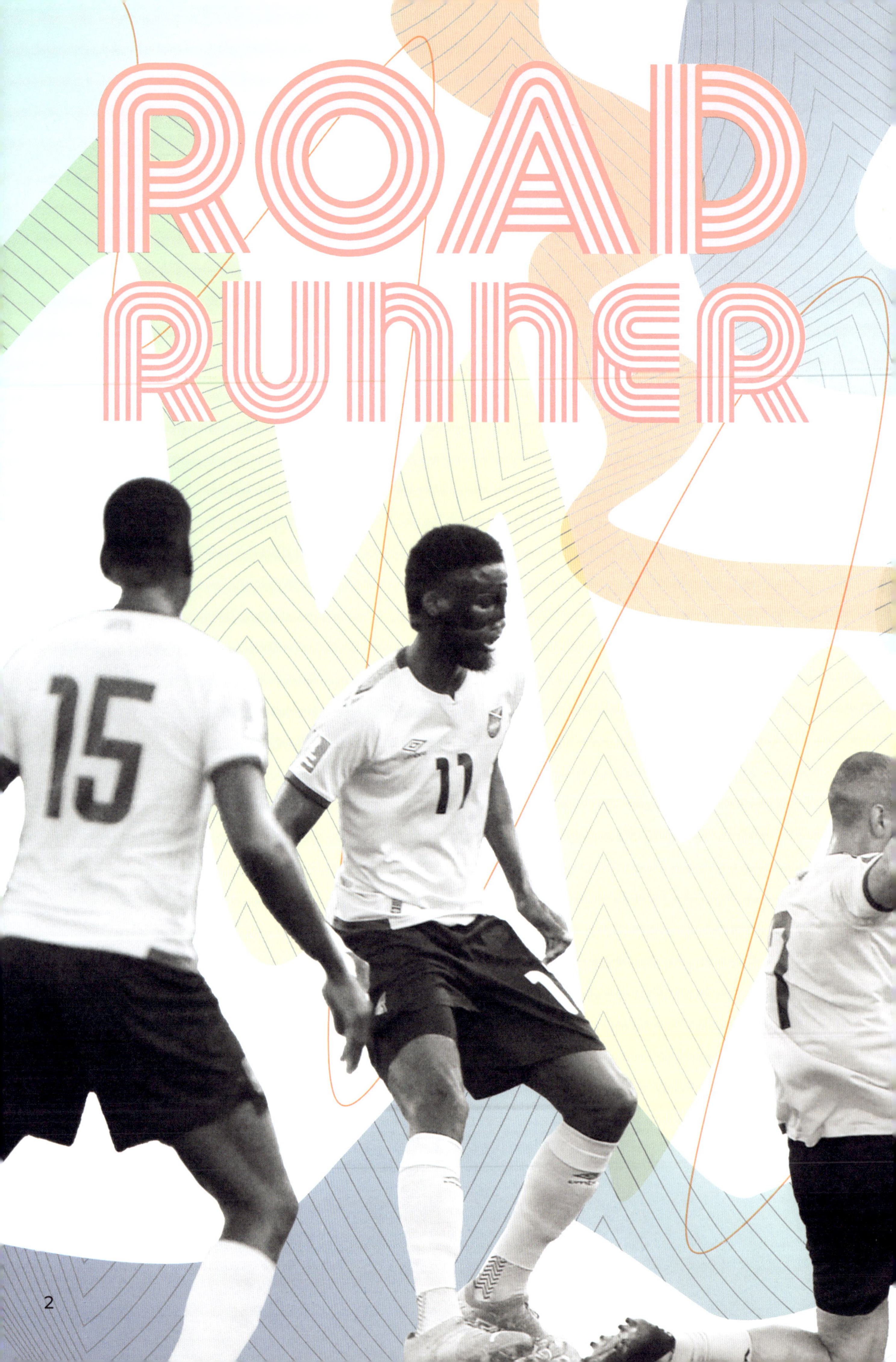

ALPHONSO DAVIES

Running running
racing racing
Phonzy Phonzy
chasing chasing
speeding speeding speeding
blurrrrring
spinning spinning spinning
swerrrrrving
dodging
sliding
tackling
stealing
dashing
zipping
like Road Runner
peeling
OUT

MEEP MEEP!

ALISSON BECKER

Alisson
Thibaut
Jan
Guillermo

leaping
reaching
sliding
blocking.

Alisson
Thibaut
Jan
Guillermo

FOUR

one hand
two hands
punching
stopping.

Alisson
Thibaut
Jan
Guillermo

JAN OBLAK

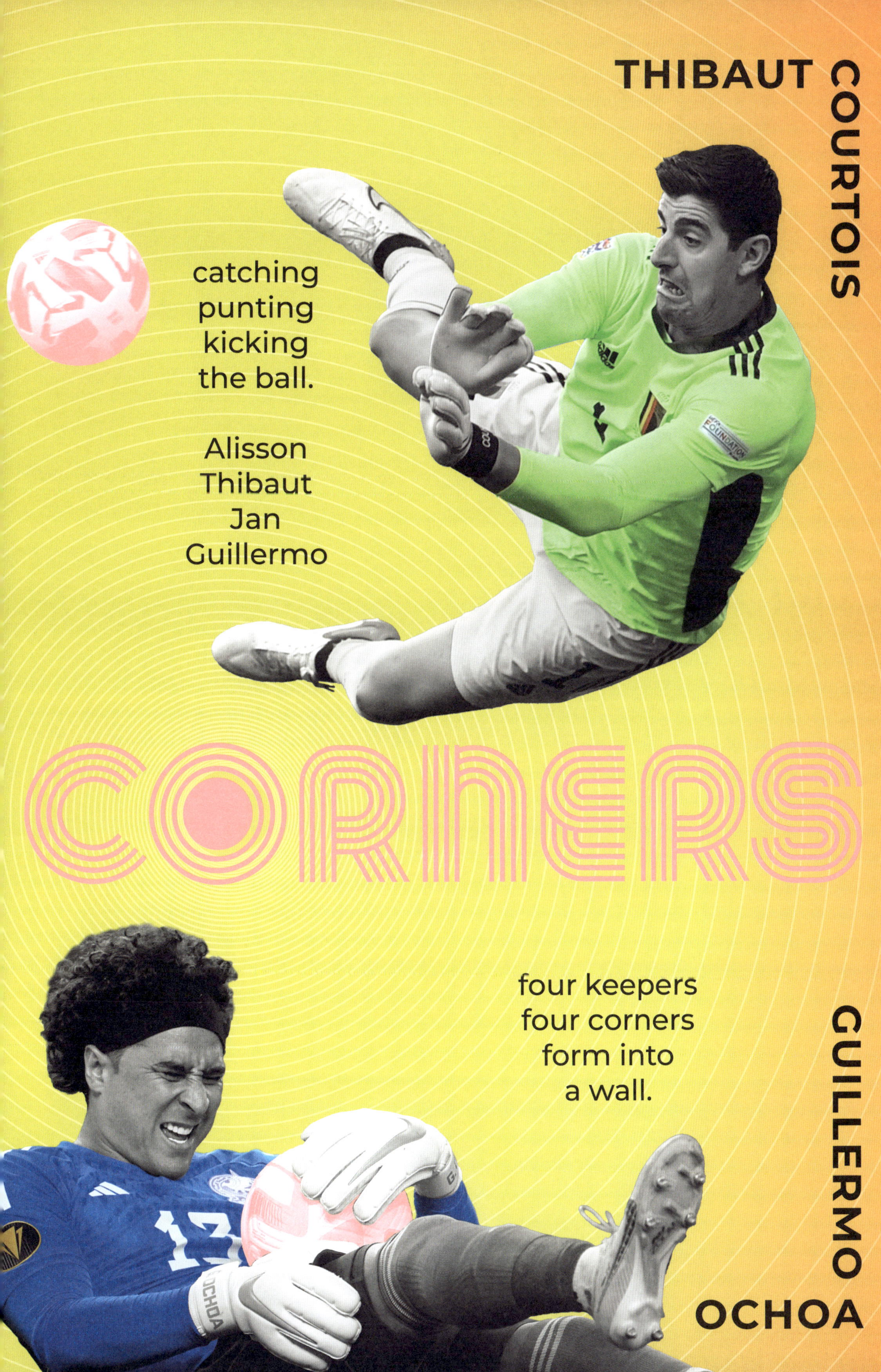
THIBAUT COURTOIS
catching
punting
kicking
the ball.
Alisson
Thibaut
Jan
Guillermo
CORNERS
four keepers
four corners
form into
a wall.
GUILLERMO OCHOA

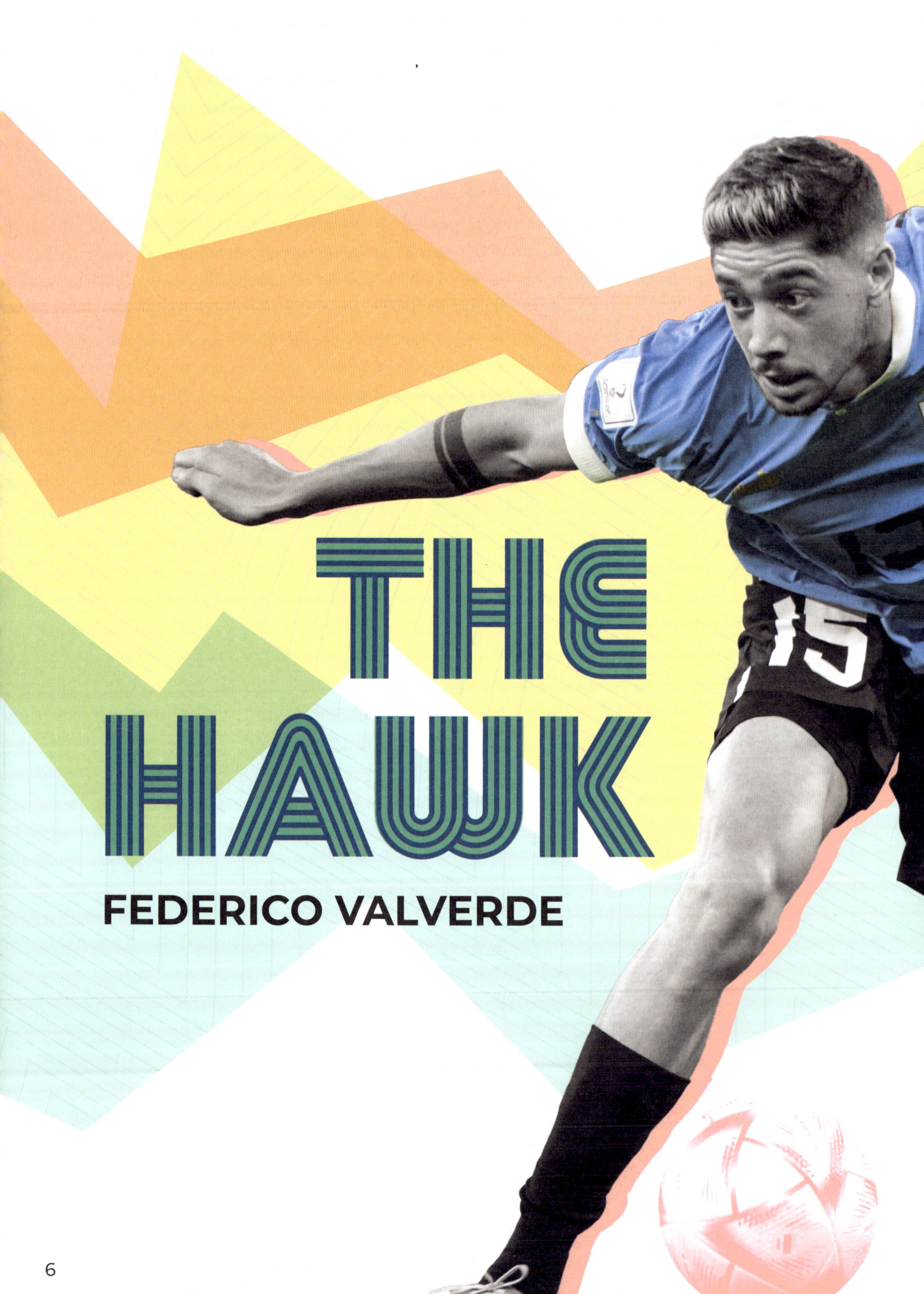

THE HAWK

FEDERICO VALVERDE

Fly
little bird,
box-to-box
across the green,
flap your wings
little bird.

Defend
your territory
your nest,
then attack
little bird.

Flap your wings,
fly,
pace your flock
through the sky,
the sky blue
little bird,
up through clouds
then emerge
as a hawk
a preying hawk
wings spread wide,
blocking out the sun
before attacking in a dive.

Focused
focused with ferocity
as you dive,
eyes wide
wings float,
you STRIKE
then fly.

Fly
hawk fly,
box-to-box
across the green,
little bird no more,
hawk,
spread your wings.

Inspired by Uruguayan folk music

THE STRIKING VIKING

ERLING HAALAND

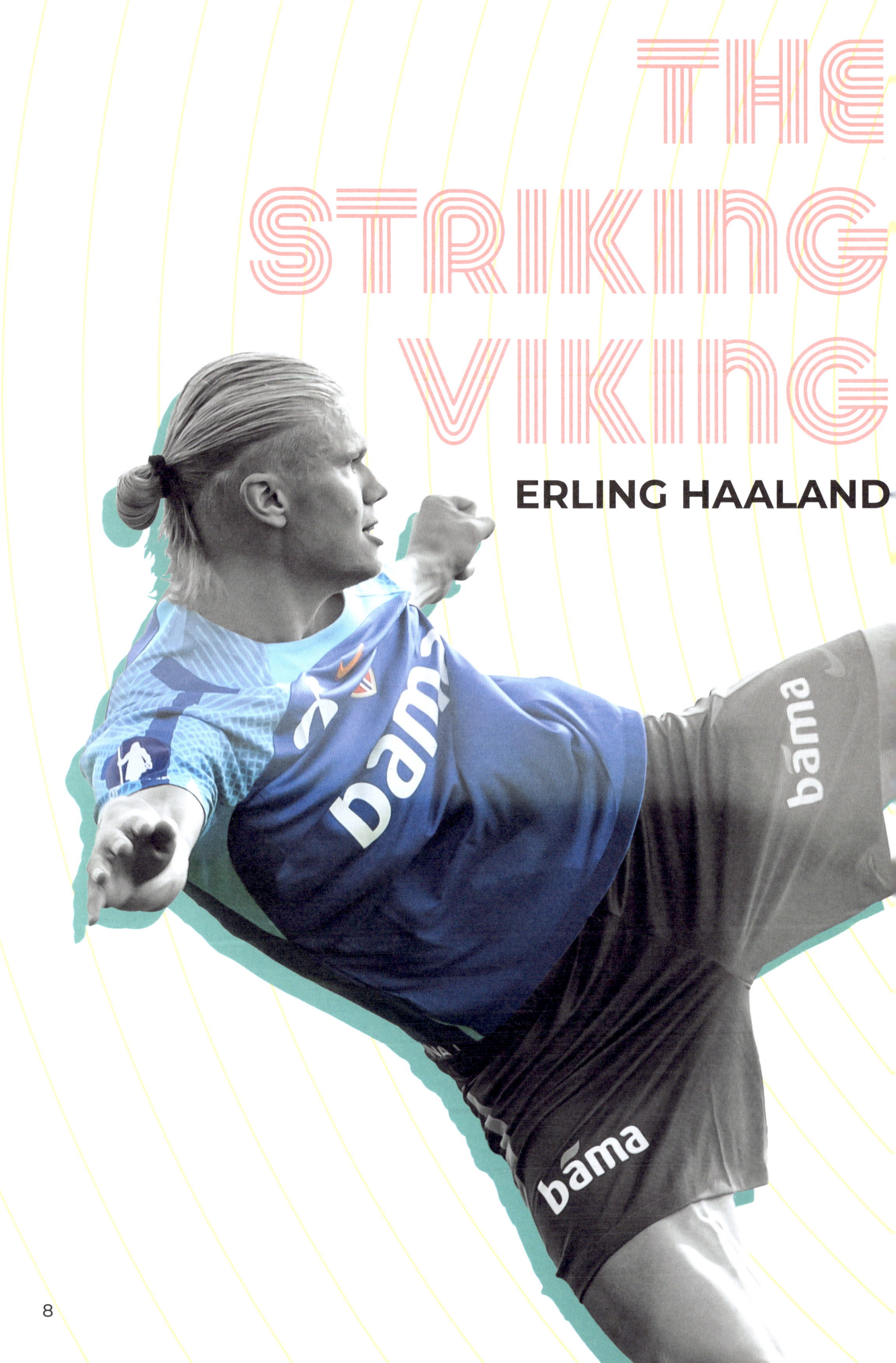

Left foot
GOAL!
Right foot
GOAL!
Speed dribble
fake
kick
GOAL!

Hat trick!

Off the head
GOAL!
Off the thigh
GOAL!
Off the chest
knee
toe
GOAL!

Hat trick!

Back heel
GOAL!
Scissor kick
GOAL!
Bottom of the boot
karate kick
GOAL!

Hat trick!

Sliding in
flying in
twisting in
chipping in
GOAL
GOAL
GOAL
GOAL!

Up close
far away
wide left
wide right
GOAL
GOAL
GOAL
GOAL!

Left corner
right corner
high
low
GOAL
GOAL
GOAL
GOAL!

Punching
spinning
bending
s
w
i
r
l
i
n
g
goals
from the Striking
Viking Erling!

Pennsylvania Pelé, from Hershey

yoUngest record breaker

Low-key leader

Instinct to attack

Smooth speedster

International prodigy

Croatian grandfather

CHRISTIAN PULISIC

Kevin
Drongen
Born

Kickstarter
De
Bruyne

Keen
Decisive
Breathtaking

Kinetic
Dime-dropping
Belgian

Keeps
Defenses
Backpedaling

Knockout
Delivering
Boot

Kicks
Driving
Blasts.

KEVIN DE BRUYNE

CHANT FOR HARRY KANE

Sung to the tune of "He's Got the Whole World in His Hands"

What's his name
what's his name?
Har-ry Kane

What's his name
what's his name?
Har-ry Kane

Harry Kane
Harry Kane,
that's his name

the best goal scorer
in the gaaame.

Harry Kane!

He's got a right foot
and a left foot
in his game

he's got a header
and a chipper
in his game

he's got power
he's got touch
in his game

the best ball striker
in the gaaame.

Harry Kane!

He's the captain
he's the captain,
Harry Kane

He's the captain
of the Lions,
Harry Kane

He's the decorated
captain,
Harry Kane

the best goal scorer
what's his name?

HARRY KANE!

THE SAM

Come Brazilians
come Brazilians
oh, Brazilians come.

To the green grass
with golden smiles
run, Brazilians run.

Bring your style
bring your skill
bring your joy,
Brazilians, come.

Samba soccer
samba soccer
samba
under the sun.

Samba Neymar
Samba Vini
Samba Paquetá
Samba Antony.

Mother Brazil needs you!

Samba
samba
samba
GO!

BA BOYS

Across the green grass
with golden smiles
Brazilians run
they run.

With joy
with passion
with speed
with style
they run
they run
they run.

Dancing
dancing
the beautiful game
in front of everyone,
samba soccer
samba soccer
samba
under the sun.

Samba Rodrygo
Samba Richarlison
Samba Raphinha
Samba Thiago.

Samba, boys
samba, boys,
samba
samba,
Samba Boys.

Dance dance
defend
attack
with style
skill
and joy!

Samba, boys
samba, boys
samba
samba,
Samba Boys,

the Canary
National Team,
mother Brazil's
pride and joy!

Inspired by Brazilian samba

LE FLO

Revving
revving
revving
waiting
number 10
accelerating
racing
racing
racing
out front
kicking
chasing
racing
out front
cornering

slaloming
steering
the ball
around
and over
slides
and shin guards,
shifting
speeding
foot on the gas,
the Blue Blur
streaking
scorches the grass,
torching the net
with an afterburn blast!

"The Blue Blur"
KYLIAN MBAPPÉ

HEUNG-MIN SON

Witness the dragon, swift and snaking, speeding,
steady and strong.
Winds whistle, waves rise, trees sway, nets tremble as
thunder echoes.
Seven Son, spirit of South Korea STRIKES,
bringing fortune.

Korean sijo

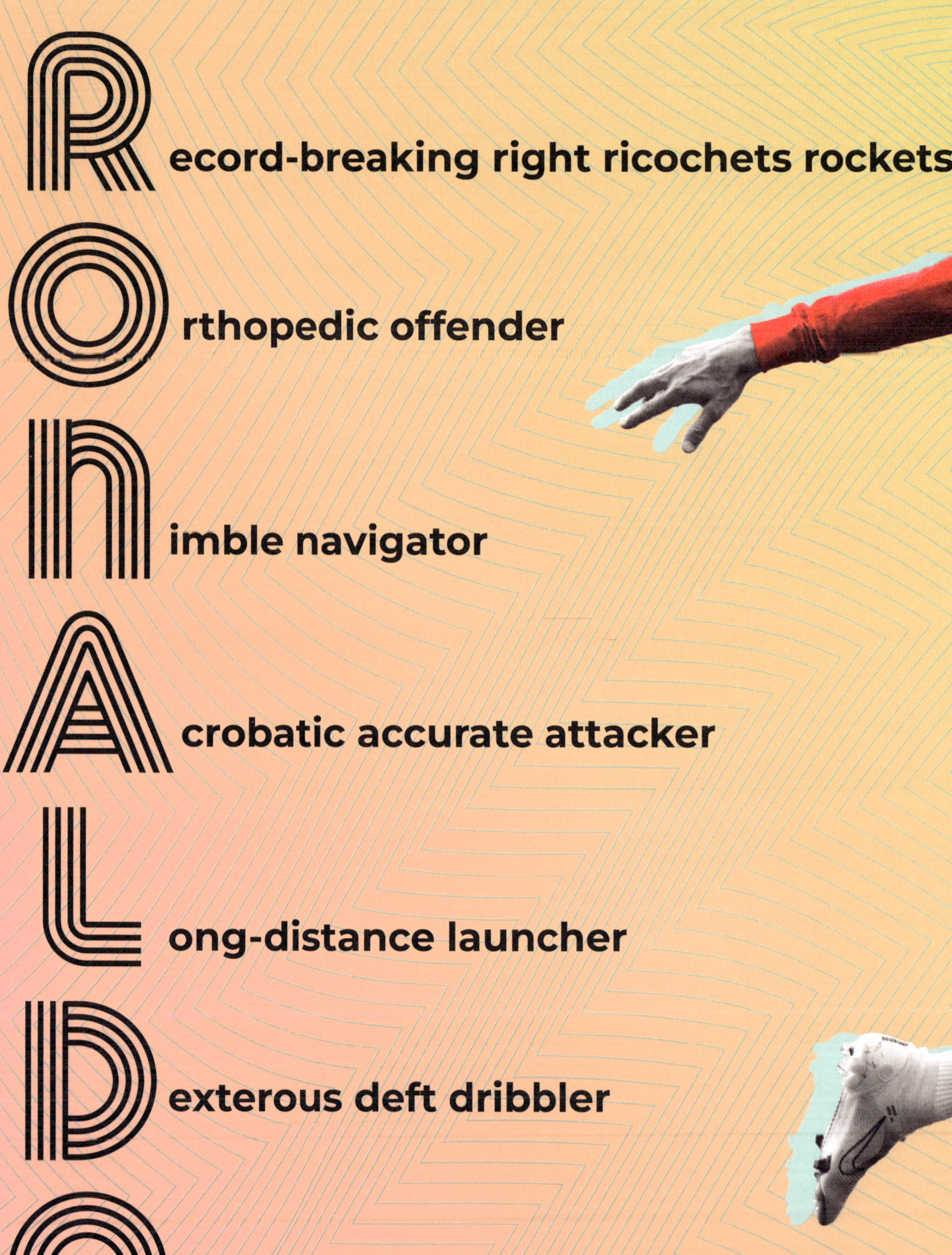

Record-breaking right ricochets rockets

Orthopedic offender

Nimble navigator

Acrobatic accurate attacker

Long-distance launcher

Dexterous deft dribbler

Outruns outjumps outlasts opponents

CRISTIANO RONALDO

Sadio Sadio
Mané,
Kalidou Kalidou
Koulibaly,
to the pitch
to the pitch
come play-yay,
Sadio
Kalidou
come play-yay.

Sadio-o-o-o-o strikes.
Sadio-o-o-o-o scores.
Kalidou-u-u-u-u stops.
Kalidou-u-u-u-u steals.

Sadio Sadio
Mané,
son of Senegal
from Bambali.

Lion of Teranga
attacking like a monster
prowling on the pitch
with ferocious
hunger,
stalking
pacing
preying
pouncing
one two three
goals scored,
announcing,
Sadio Sadio
Mané,
son of Senegal
from Bambali.

Sadio-o-o-o-o strikes.
Sadio-o-o-o-o scores.
Sadio-o-o-o-o strikes.
Sadio-o-o-o-o scores.

Kalidou Kalidou
where are you,
Kalidou Koulibaly
whatchu gonna do?
Son of Senegal
born in France,
Captain Koulibaly
make your grand entrance.

Lion of Teranga
attacking like a monster
protecting his brothers
with ferocious
hunger,
stalking
marking
tackling
stealing
stealing
stealing
keeping crowds cheering
the son of Senegal,
Captain Koulibaly
Captain Kalidou
Kalidou Koulibaly.

Kalidou-u-u-u-u stops.
Kalidou-u-u-u-u steals.
Kalidou-u-u-u-u stops.
Kalidou-u-u-u-u steals.

Sadio-o-o-o-o strikes.
Sadio-o-o-o-o scores.
Kalidou-u-u-u-u steals.
Sadio-o-o-o-o scores.

Senegal-al-al-al-al WINS!

Inspired by Afrobeat music

LIONS

SADIO MANÉ & KALIDOU KOULIBALY

THE

Samba soccer
samba soccer
what oh what is
samba soccer?

Show them Neymar
samba soccer
show them, maestro,
how to play,
samba soccer
show them, Neymar,
SAMBA

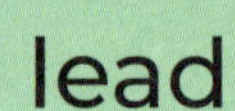

lead

the

way.

Magical feet
so sweet
stepping to
a samba beat
step-step
spin-spinning
defenders to the grouuuund.

MAESTRO

NEYMAR

Moving
and grooving
and grooving
and grooving
and moving
shaking
taking
making
goals with your own sound.

Neyyy-marrr
Neymar hey-hey!

Samba samba
samba samba
hey-hey Neymar
samba soccer.

Neyyy-marrr
Neymar hey hey!

Neymar-Neymar
lead the way
samba soccer
samba, hey!

Inspired by Brazilian samba

THE EAGLE

ROBERT LEWANDOWSKI

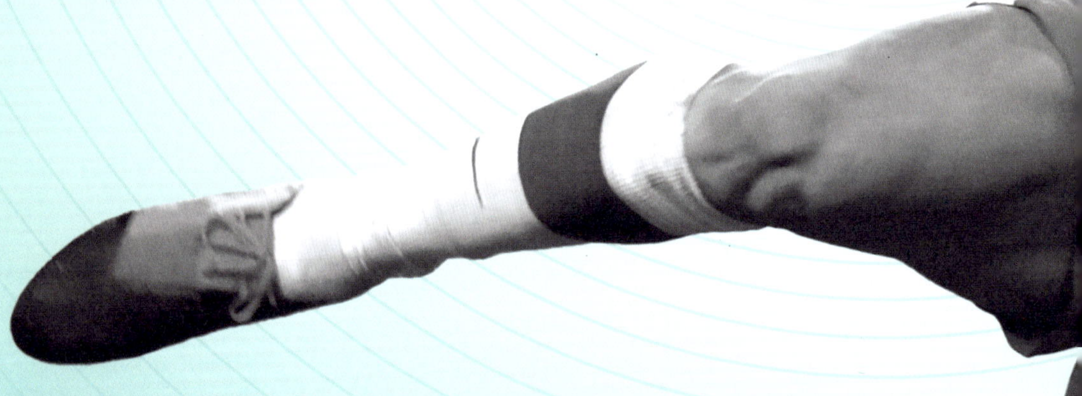

Warsaw's world wonder, Poland's white-tailed eagle,
unflappable, calm, with bearing so regal,
attacks nets like prey, standing fans up to see,
GOALLLL, Lewan-GOAL-ski!

Polish Sapphic stanza

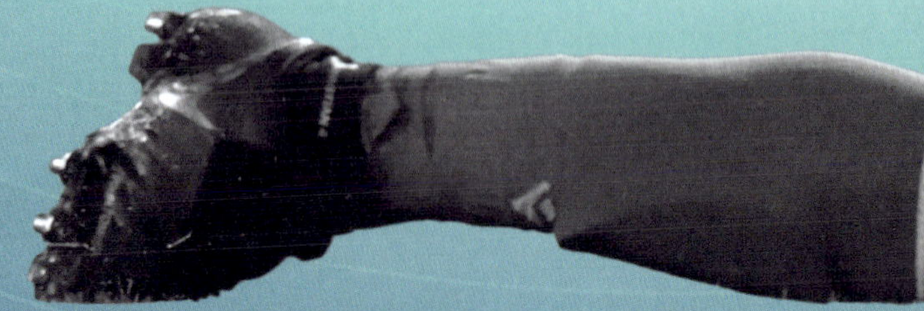

Majestic Mohamed Salah, we cheer with all those who sing
praises of you, the humble, true king.

Witness speedy Mo, gusting past defenders
like a sirocco wind sweeping through spring.

Slippery, sly, skillful Salah,
like the tail of a scorpion, opponents, you sting.

Salah, Mo Salah, known to break hearts,
enough to make a shoe fling.

So says me, Charles, a mere poet, blessed to witness
the Egyptian King, and all the joy you do bring.

Arabic ghazal

MOHAMED SALAH

TIAN KING

THE MA

Here he comes
here he comes
Lio Messi
on the run,
slippery
and slick
zigzagging
and quick,
darting and
dodging and
dancing with ease
splitting legs
dropping
defenders to their knees.
Messi Messi
the mercurial magician
on a goal-scoring mission
disappearing
reappearing
with sleight of foot precision,
little Lio causing
collision
after collision,
faking
feinting
focused
and fearless,
Lio's
LEFT FOOT
leaves the crowd breathless.

GICIAN
LIONEL MESSI

VIRGIL

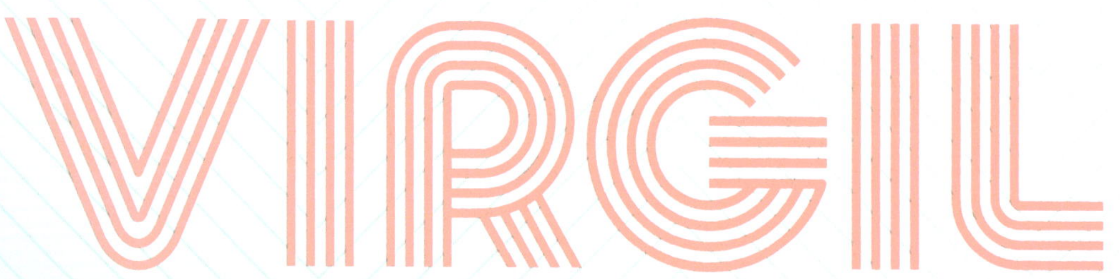

VIRGIL VAN DIJK

1) Versatile

2) vocal

3) valuable

4) veteran

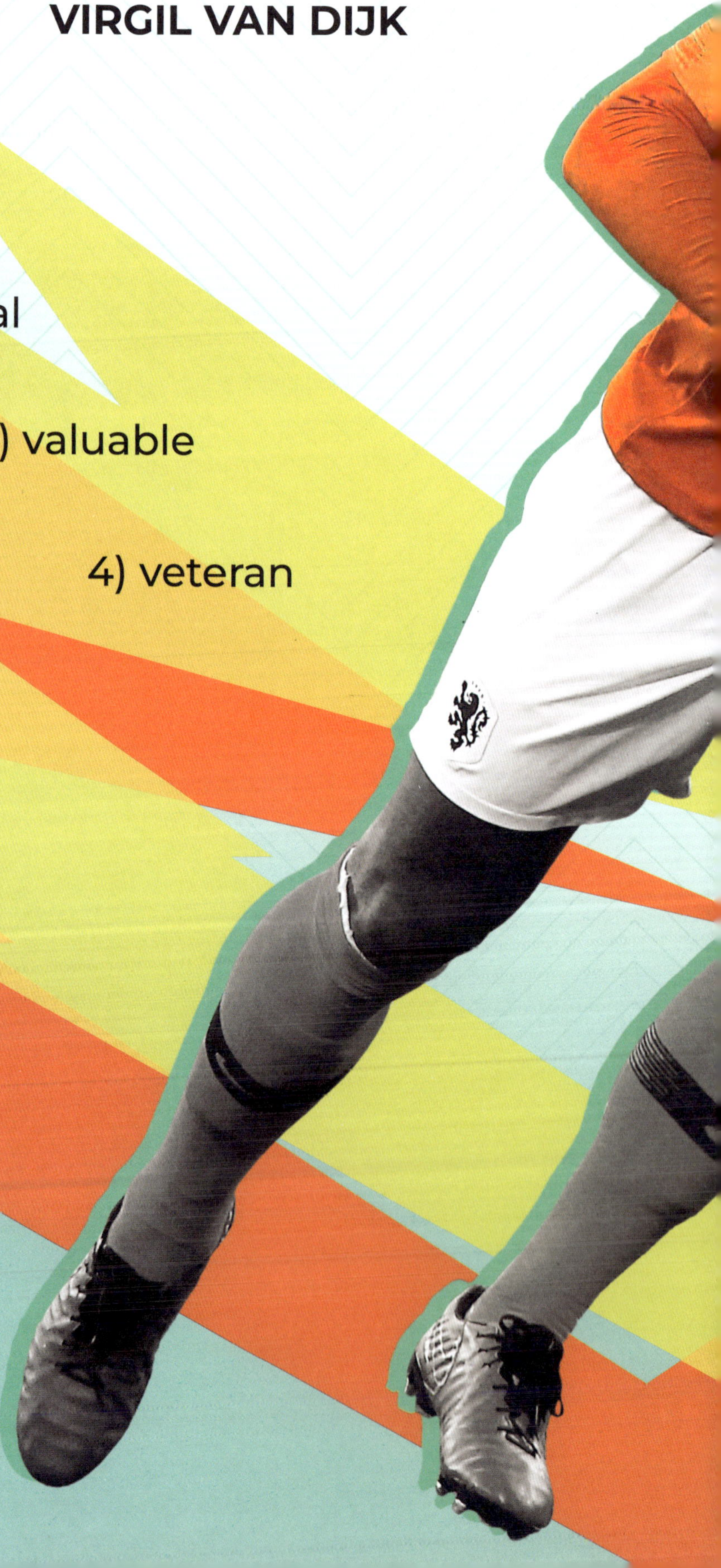

9) Victorious!

8) valiantly.

7) virtuosos

6) vaporizing

5) vexes

PLAYER NOTES

Alphonso Davies
Alphonso's nickname is Road Runner because he is usually the fastest on the pitch. Off the field he's known as Phonzy. His poem was my favorite to research because I watched lots of video of him as well as classic Road Runner cartoons. This helped me describe how he uses his speed and creativity.

Alisson Becker, Thibaut Courtois, Jan Oblak, Guillermo Ochoa
These four goalkeepers are some of the best, and each has his own style. But what they all have in common is the ability to become a wall for their team when they need it. To show this, I described the different ways they stop the ball. I then created a rhythm by repeating each of their names to tie them and their shared job together.

Federico Valverde
He was probably the toughest player to write about since he can do it all and make it look so easy. When a player has Fede's skills, he's known as a box-to-box player. This means he can go from defense to offense with speed and ease. Since he has too many skills to choose from, I decided to focus instead on his nickname. As a young player, Fede was known as Pajarito, which means *birdie*, because he was so slight and small. But after a big game where he showed great skill and growth, his nickname changed to Halcón, which means *hawk*. In his poem, I show that change happening as he goes from defense to offense. The style also takes inspiration from Uruguayan folk music, which uses storytelling with repetition accompanied by a guitar.

Erling Haaland
This striker from Norway can score from anywhere, at any time, on anyone. Watching him play, I simply wrote of the various ways I witnessed him score. Viking culture is honored and celebrated in Norway, earning him the rhyming nickname.

Christian Pulisic
Christian's last name comes from his Croatian heritage, so I used an acrostic for those letters. Playing against international competition at a young age, Christian caught the eyes of scouts from some of the world's best teams. By the age of sixteen he turned pro, joining a German team, and broke every kind of record for an American by age each time he scored or won.

Kevin De Bruyne
Born in Drongen, Belgium, Kevin De Bruyne is often called simply KDB. I focused on those three letters to create mini acrostics. Since seven is his number on the Belgium team, I used seven acrostics to describe his versatile game.

Harry Kane
Soccer chants are popular in British stadiums and wherever the English team plays. The chants usually use a familiar melody so that it's easy to follow, and "He's Got the Whole World in His Hands" is one of the most popular. The English team's nickname is the Three Lions, and as team captain, Harry won a Golden Boot, which is awarded to the player who scores the most goals during a World Cup.

The Samba Boys
Brazil was the most fun to write about since they play using such a unique style. They call it samba soccer because the players move with a samba rhythm, in which fast drumming leads to quick-moving feet. The Brazilian flag has a blue disk on a background of green and gold. The green represents the nation's forests, while the gold represents wealth. The Brazil national team has several nicknames, including Seleção Canarinho (the Canary Team), and its players take pride in wearing the canary yellow and green.

Kylian Mbappé
Formula 1 racing is very popular in France, and since Kylian Mbappé is as fast as a race car, I wrote the poem as if he were a car in a race, beginning when he gets the ball and ending with him scoring the goal. I called him the Blue Blur because the French team's nickname is Les Bleus, or the Blues.

Heung-Min Son
In Korea, the dragon is a symbol of fortune, luck, and blessings. When Heung-Min Son has the ball at his feet, racing on the pitch, he moves like a dragon to bring fortune in the form of a goal. I chose to celebrate his game and country using a Korean poetic form called a sijo, which you can learn more about in the Poetic Forms section.

Cristiano Ronaldo
Most people know this player by one name. Ronaldo's array of skills are showcased by what I call a multiple acrostic. That means multiple words with the same first letter are used to spell out his name.

Sadio Mané & Kalidou Koulibaly
I had so much fun writing this poem and am excited to perform it live. It takes its rhythm from Afrobeat music, with its heavy drums and repeated words. Sadio Mané and Kalidou Koulibaly play very different positions for Senegal. Sadio attacks and Kalidou defends. Afrobeats and

traditional Senegalese music often use call-and-response, where one person or instrument makes a statement, and another responds by repeating it and adding a twist. In this case, I focused on Sadio scoring goals on one end of the pitch and Kalidou stopping them on the other. The Senegalese team is called the Lions of Teranga, so I used the metaphor of them as lions, with Sadio as the main aggressor and Kalidou as the protector. Sadio is very proud of where he is from and has supported his hometown of Bambali by founding a hospital, a school, and other resources. Kalidou was born in France, but his parents are from Senegal, so I wanted to show that connection.

Neymar
The Brazilian team always features some of the best world talent, and Neymar is the best of the best. Playing multiple positions, he leads the team like a conductor leads an orchestra.

Robert Lewandowski
The celebrated Polish striker known as "Lewan-goal-ski" was born in Warsaw. I chose to compare him to an eagle, the symbol of Poland. The poem is written in a specific type of verse called a Sapphic stanza. You can learn more about it in the Poetic Forms section.

Mohamed Salah
Small in size but big in game, Egyptian player Mohamed "Mo" Salah has been nicknamed the Egyptian King, so I wanted to show why he's considered a king at this game. Because he uses his speed to score, I compared him to a sirocco, a hot desert wind unique to Egypt and North Africa that's known to be quick-moving, speeding fastest in spring. To honor his heritage, I used an Arabic poetic form called a ghazal. The form was one of the toughest for me to follow, requiring me to mention myself, but it made for a great poem. Check out the ghazal in the Poetic Forms section.

Lionel Messi
Arguably the greatest footballer of all time, Lionel Messi is a sight to see on the pitch. One of his nicknames is the Magician because of how he disappears from defenders with ease. Before you know it, he reappears, dribbling the ball, ready to launch another goal with his lethal left foot.

Virgil van Dijk
Whenever an athlete's name starts with a unique letter, I try to do something with that. In Virgil's case, I made a V-shaped poem and only used words that start with that letter. But I still wanted the words to tell a story. And in nine words I was able to sum up Virgil's strengths and, uh, value.

POETIC FORMS

Ghazal (guh-zl)
This Arabic form was embraced early on by medieval Persian poets. It has a minimum of five couplets. Each couplet, which is two lines, should be able to stand on its own, and each line should attempt to be the same length. In the first couplet, the last two words of both lines must rhyme. The second line in all the remaining couplets must also match the rhyme from the first couplet. The first line of the last couplet mentions the speaker.

Sounds complicated, right? It is, but all the rules create a natural rhythm and make for a fun-to-read poem. Take a look at "The Egyptian King" to see the rules at work:

In the first couplet the ends of both lines rhyme, but not just the last word in each line. The last two words must rhyme.

> Majestic Mohamed Salah, we cheer with all those *who sing*
> praises of you, the humble, *true king.*

After the first couplet, each second line rhymes with the first couplet.

> Witness speedy Mo, gusting past defenders
> like a sirocco wind sweeping *through spring.*
>
> Slippery, sly, skillful Salah,
> like the tail of a scorpion, opponents, *you sting.*
>
> Salah, Mo Salah, known to break hearts,
> enough to make a *shoe fling.*

The first line of the last couplet mentions the speaker.

> So says me, Charles, a mere poet, blessed to witness
> the Egyptian King, and all the joy you *do bring.*

If you enjoyed this poem, check out other ghazals by the poet Rumi.

Sijo (SHEE-joh)

The sijo originated in Korea. It is made up of three lines total, with between fourteen and sixteen syllables per line. Each line usually has a syllable pattern of 3-4-4-4. This does not mean each word has to have that many syllables. It means the words should be able to be separated without being broken.

First line example from "Sijo for Son":

> Witness the (3) / dragon, swift and (4) / snaking, speeding, (4) /
> steady and strong. (4)

Sapphic Stanza

Though the Sapphic stanza has its origins in Latin and Greek, many Polish poets have embraced the form. It is made up of four lines, the first three of which have eleven syllables each, while the last has only five. The eleven syllables are broken down into 5 + 6. That means the words should be able to be separated into those syllables without being broken. The last words of the first and second lines rhyme, as do the last words of the third and fourth lines.

It's not as complicated as it sounds. The tricky part is the last line with just five syllables. Take a look at "The Eagle" to see how the poem breaks down:

> Warsaw's world wonder, (5) / Poland's white-tailed eagle, (6)
> unflappable, calm, (5) / with bearing so regal, (6)
> attacks nets like prey, (5) / standing fans up to see, (6)
> GOALLLL, Lewan-GOAL-ski! (5)

Dedicated to my dog, Jake, who was there through each line and each rhyme

Text copyright © 2026 by Charles R. Smith Jr.

Photography Credits
pp. 2–3: copyright © 2021 by AP/Collin Reid
p. 4 (top): copyright © 2024 by AP/Tony Avelar
p. 4 (bottom): copyright © 2021 by AP
p. 5 (top): copyright © 2021 by Sipa USA via AP/Dirk Waem
p. 5 (bottom): copyright © 2023 by AP/David J. Phillip
pp. 6–7: copyright © 2022 by Sipa USA via AP/Andrew Surma
pp. 8–9: copyright © 2023 by Sipa USA via AP/Bildbyran
pp. 10–11: copyright © 2023 by AP/John Raoux
pp. 12–13: copyright © 2024 by Sipa USA via AP/David Catry
pp. 14–15: copyright © 2024 by AP/Martin Meissner
pp. 16–17: copyright © 2022 by AP/Pavel Golovkin
pp. 18–19: copyright © 2024 by Sipa USA via AP/FEP
pp. 20–21: copyright © 2024 by Sipa USA via AP/Amphol Thongmueangluang/SOPA Images
pp. 22–23: copyright © 2022 by AP/Laurent Gillieron
p. 24: copyright © 2022 by AP/Themba Hadebe
p. 25: copyright © 2022 by Sipa USA via AP/Pro Shots Photo Agency
pp. 26–27: copyright © 2021 by Sipa USA via AP/MB Media
pp. 28–29: copyright © 2021 by AP/Czarek Sokolowski
pp. 30–31: copyright © 2022 by AP/Amr Nabil
pp. 32–33: copyright © 2023 by AP/Federico Peretti/NurPhoto
pp. 34–35: copyright © 2019 by firo Sportphoto/Ralf Ibing/picture-alliance/dpa/AP Images

All rights reserved. No part of this book may be reproduced, transmitted, or stored in an information retrieval system in any form or by any means, graphic, electronic, or mechanical, including photocopying, taping, and recording, without prior written permission from the publisher. Additionally, no part of this book may be used or reproduced in any manner for the purpose of training artificial intelligence technologies or systems, nor for text and data mining.

First edition 2026

Library of Congress Control Number: pending
ISBN 978-1-5362-3487-9 (hardcover)
ISBN 978-1-5362-5224-8 (paperback)

25 26 27 28 29 30 CCP 10 9 8 7 6 5 4 3 2 1

Printed in Shenzhen, Guangdong, China

This book was typeset in Montserrat.
Digital artwork and typography by Tif Bucknor.

Candlewick Press
99 Dover Street
Somerville, Massachusetts 02144

www.candlewick.com

EU Authorized Representative:
HackettFlynn Ltd, 36 Cloch Choirneal,
Balrothery, Co. Dublin, K32 C942, Ireland.
EU@walkerpublishinggroup.com

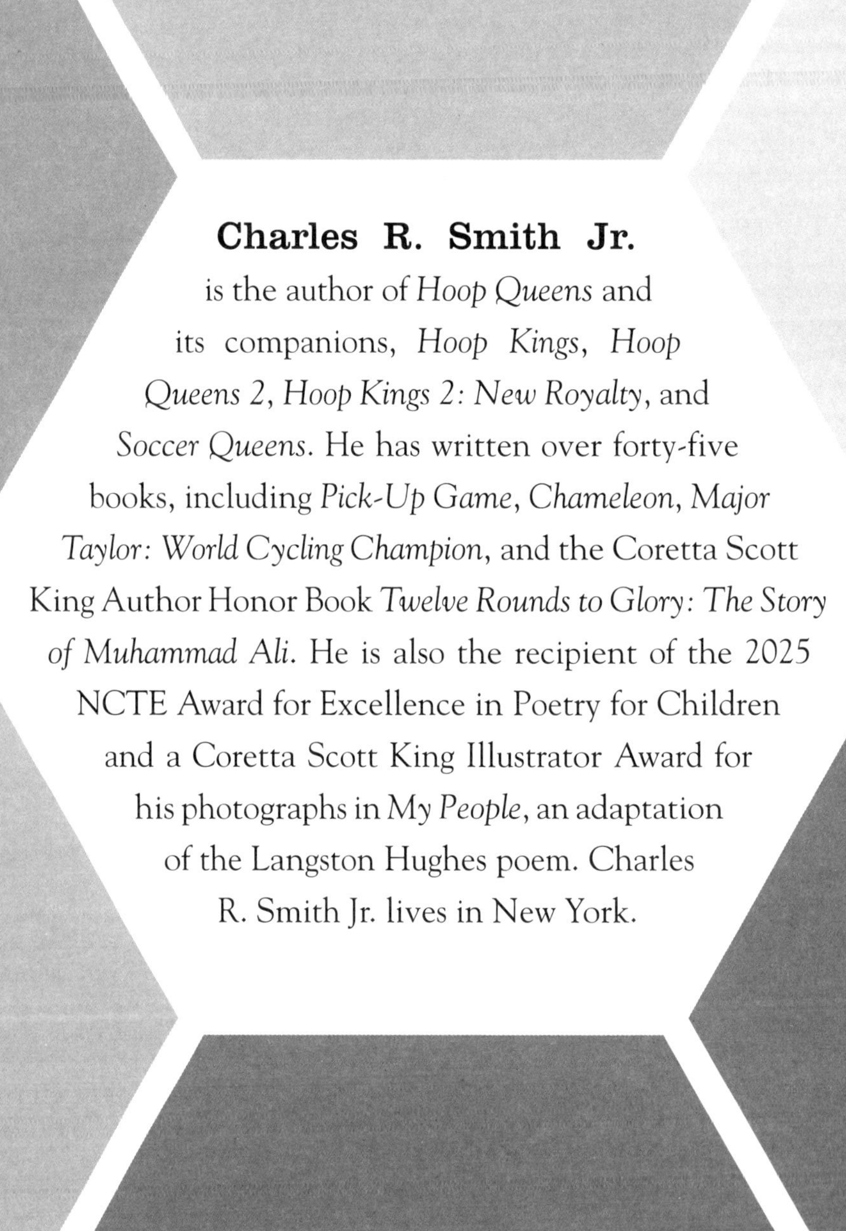

Charles R. Smith Jr. is the author of *Hoop Queens* and its companions, *Hoop Kings*, *Hoop Queens 2*, *Hoop Kings 2: New Royalty*, and *Soccer Queens*. He has written over forty-five books, including *Pick-Up Game*, *Chameleon*, *Major Taylor: World Cycling Champion*, and the Coretta Scott King Author Honor Book *Twelve Rounds to Glory: The Story of Muhammad Ali*. He is also the recipient of the 2025 NCTE Award for Excellence in Poetry for Children and a Coretta Scott King Illustrator Award for his photographs in *My People*, an adaptation of the Langston Hughes poem. Charles R. Smith Jr. lives in New York.